the Magical Unicorn cookbook

by Nicola Graimes

SCHOLASTIC

Published in the UK by Scholastic Children's Books, 2021
Euston House, 24 Eversholt Street, London, NW1 1DB
A division of Scholastic Limited

London ~ New York ~ Toronto ~ Sydney ~ Auckland
Mexico City ~ New Delhi ~ Hong Kong

Scholastic Ltd., Ireland Offices at: Unit 89E, Lagan Road,
Dublin Industrial Estate, Glasnevin, Dublin 11

SCHOLASTIC and associated logos are trademarks and/or
registered trademarks of Scholastic Inc.

Author: Nicola Graimes
Text © Scholastic Children's Books, 2021
Photography © Scholastic Children's Books, 2021

Recipes and Styling: Nicola Graimes
Food Styling: Anneli Fleming-Brown
Photography: Xavier D. Buendia
Senior Designer: Aimee Stewart

Trade hardback edition ISBN 978 0702 31118 5

A CIP catalogue record for this book is available from the British Library.

Printed by L.E.G.O. S.p.A., Italy

Papers used by Scholastic Children's Books are made
from wood grown in sustainable forests.

1 3 5 7 9 10 8 6 4 2

www.scholastic.co.uk

Contents

Baking Basics

Enjoy your magical baking adventure with this collection of unicorn and rainbow cakes, biscuits, pastries and breads. Here are a few basics to get you started...

Before you start baking...

1. Check the ingredients for each recipe carefully if you have a food allergy or a special dietary requirement.

2. Always wash your hands and put on an apron to protect your clothes.

3. Be safe – always ask an adult before you start cooking. Take extra care when handling anything hot, sharp or electrical and ask an adult to help. Use oven gloves when handling hot tins and trays.

4. Read the recipe in full. Each recipe in the book comes with a full list of instructions. You should ask an adult for help with these recipes when you are in the kitchen.

5. Weigh and measure all the ingredients carefully before you start. Weigh dry ingredients on kitchen scales and use a measuring jug or spoon for liquids.

6. Make sure you have the right size cakes tins, trays and cake cases mentioned in the recipe. Prepare your tin, tray and cases before you start.

7. Heat the oven for 15 to 20 minutes before baking to give it time to reach the correct temperature.

8. Don't forget to clean up afterwards, mop up any spills and help by doing the washing-up!

Vanilla Buttercream

Creamy, fluffy buttercream is a popular cake topping and filling and is used in many of the recipes in this book. It can also be coloured and/or flavoured and is perfect for piping.

Makes: enough for 12 cupcakes
You will need:
✦ 175g unsalted butter, softened ✦ 1 teaspoon vanilla extract ✦ Pinch of salt ✦ 300g icing sugar, sifted
✦ 1–2 tablespoons whole milk (optional)

1. Put the softened butter in the bowl of a stand mixer with the beater attachment. (Alternatively, use an electric hand whisk or wooden spoon.)

2. Beat until creamy, then add the vanilla extract, salt and the icing sugar in two batches. Continue to beat for 3 minutes until light and fluffy. (See image on the bottom left of page 5.)

3. Beat in the milk, if needed, starting with the smaller amount. Keep for up to three days in the fridge or freeze for up to three months.

Unicorn Decorations

A unicorn wouldn't be a unicorn without a horn, ears and eyes! Here are some tips to help you decorate your unicorn cakes and bakes.

You will need:

✦ Icing sugar, for dusting ✦ White fondant icing ✦ Edible gold powder (optional)
✦ Gel food colouring of choice

Unicorn ears:

1. To make the fondant ears, dust a worktop with icing sugar. Using a small rolling pin, roll out the fondant icing, about 3–4mm thick.

2. Cut out two ear shapes with a rounded top and a straight bottom, about 4cm high for large unicorn ears, 2.5cm high for medium and 1.5cm for smaller ones. (See image on the bottom right of the page.)

3. Using a damp paint brush, brush a little edible gold powder over the inner part of each ear, then pinch the bottom slightly together. Leave to set for a few hours, or overnight.

Unicorn horns:

1. First colour your fondant by adding a few drops of your chosen food colouring to the quantity of fondant given in the recipe, then knead in the colour until evenly mixed in.

2. Divide the fondant into pieces and roll each one into a cylinder. Now, shape each piece into a cone shape with a wider base and narrowing to a pointed tip, slightly twisting the fondant to give a ridged horn effect. (See image on the bottom middle of the page.)

3. Leave to harden for a few hours, or overnight. Attach the horn, using either the buttercream coating to hold it in place or with a blob of edible glue. Brush the horns with a little edible gold powder, if liked, to finish.

Unicorn eyes:

Unicorn eyes can be made out of black fondant, black card or drawn on with edible black pen or black writing icing. Have fun creating your own favourite shape!

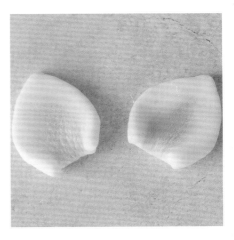

Magical
biscuits & bites

Unicorn cake pops

If you have any leftover cake, then what better way to use it up than these cute unicorn cake pops? They're so fun to make!

Makes: about 8 (depending on size)
Preparation: 2 hours, plus chilling

You will need:

+ 200g cake offcuts

+ 60g Vanilla Buttercream (make ¼ quantity, see page 4)

To decorate:

+ Icing sugar, for dusting

+ 400g ready-made white fondant icing

+ Edible glue

+ Coloured sugar strand sprinkles

+ Silver balls

+ Orange gel food colouring

+ Edible gold powder

+ Black writing icing or edible black pen

Special equipment:

+ 1 large baking tray

+ Baking paper

Top Tip!
You could use a shop-bought sponge to make these cake pops.

1. Line a baking tray with baking paper.

2. Put the cake offcuts in a food processor and blitz to fine crumbs. Tip the cake crumbs into a mixing bowl, then mix in the buttercream until combined. Using your hands, roll the mixture into eight balls, each about the size of a walnut. Place the balls on the lined baking tray and chill for 30 minutes to firm up.

3. Lightly dust a work top with icing sugar. Roll out 300g of the fondant icing until about 2mm thick and cut out eight 10cm diameter rounds.

4. Place one ball in the centre of a fondant round. Using your hands, shape the fondant tightly around the ball and press together the edges until the ball is covered in fondant. Trim off any excess fondant and repeat to make eight fondant-covered balls.

5. To make the horns, colour 32g fondant icing with a few drops of orange colouring, kneading it in until evenly coloured. Divide into eight 4g pieces and roll each one into a cylinder, about 3.5cm long. Shape each piece into a horn, twisting it to give a ridged effect. Place a blob of edible glue on the top of each ball and attach the horns, pressing them down slightly. Brush the horns with gold powder, then leave to set.

6. To make the ears, roll out the remaining icing until about 4mm thick. Cut out 16 ears, about 1.5cm high with a flat base. Paint a little edible gold powder in the centre of each ear and pinch the bottom together slightly. Brush glue on the bottom of the ears and attach to either side of each horn. Leave for 30 minutes.

7. Using writing icing or edible pen, draw two black unicorn eyes with lashes on the front of each ball.

8. To make the unicorn mane, brush a little edible glue over the top of each ball, scatter over some sprinkles and press on a few silver balls to finish. Leave to set for 30 minutes.

✦·⭒ Fairy Dust Florentines ⭒·✦

These teeny, fairy-sized biscuits are sprinkled with dried strawberry pieces,
pink candy hearts and a magical glittery fairy dust.

Makes: about 26
Preparation: 30 minutes,
plus cooling
Bake: 12 minutes

You will need:

+ 60g flaked almonds
+ 50g plain flour
+ Pinch of salt
+ 50g unsalted butter
+ 50g golden syrup
+ 50g caster sugar
+ 115g milk chocolate

To decorate:

+ Freeze-dried strawberry pieces
+ Pink candy hearts
+ Edible pink glitter dust

Special equipment:

+ 2 large baking trays
+ Baking paper

Top Tip!

Stir your favourite chopped dried fruit — apricots, dates, raisins — into the biscuit mix.

1. Heat the oven to 180C/160C fan/Gas 4 and line two baking trays with baking paper.

2. Roughly chop half the almonds and put them in a large mixing bowl with the rest of the almonds. Stir in the flour and salt.

3. Melt the butter, golden syrup and sugar in a small pan over a medium-low heat. Stir with a wooden spoon for 2 to 3 minutes until the sugar dissolves. Pour the mixture into the mixing bowl with the almond mixture and mix together with a wooden spoon.

4. Using a teaspoon, place 24 heaped round mounds of the mixture onto the lined baking trays, spacing them well apart as they spread during baking. Bake for 10 to 12 minutes until light golden, then carefully remove from the oven. Leave on the tray for 10 minutes, then place on a wire rack to cool completely.

5. Break the milk chocolate into even-sized pieces and place in a heatproof bowl. Set the bowl over a small pan of gently simmering water, making sure the bottom of the bowl does not touch the water. Gently melt the chocolate, stirring a couple of times.

6. Turn the florentines over on the rack, so the smooth side is facing upwards. Spoon the chocolate over the top of each one. Using the back of a teaspoon, spread the chocolate out slightly. Decorate with dried strawberries, candy hearts and a sprinkling of glitter, then leave the chocolate to set.

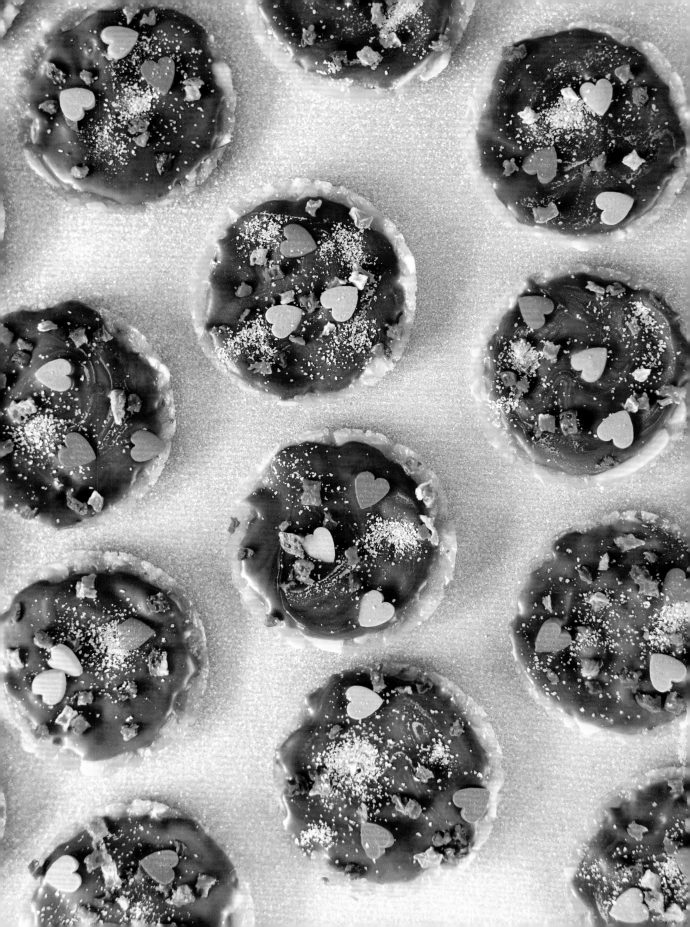

Glittery butterflies

These buttery, fluttery shortbread biscuits are speckled with colourful sprinkles.
Have fun decorating them with sparkly edible glitter, too!

Makes: about 18 (depending on size)
Preparation: 30 minutes, plus cooling
Bake: 20 minutes

You will need:

✦ 250g plain flour, plus extra for dusting

✦ 25g cornflour

✦ 75g caster sugar

✦ 175g unsalted butter, chilled and cut into pieces

✦ 1 teaspoon whole milk

✦ 2 tablespoons bright coloured sprinkles

To decorate:

✦ Edible glitter pen and glitter

✦ Shaped sprinkles

Special equipment:

✦ 2 large baking trays

✦ Butterfly pastry cutters (two sizes)

✦ Baking paper

Top Tip!
Use your favourite cutters to make different shapes.

1. Heat the oven to 180C/160C fan/Gas 4 and line two baking trays with baking paper.

2. Sift the flour, cornflour and caster sugar into a large mixing bowl and mix together. Using your fingertips, rub in the butter to make a soft, crumbly, buttery mixture.

3. Using a wooden spoon, stir in the milk and sprinkles until combined, then bring the mixture together with your hands into a smooth ball of dough.

4. Lightly flour the work surface and roll out the dough to 5mm thick. Using the cutters, stamp out butterfly shapes, re-rolling the dough when needed.

5. Arrange the biscuits on the baking trays, spaced slightly apart, and bake for 15 to 20 minutes until pale golden and crisp underneath. Leave the biscuits to cool for 5 minutes on the tray, then place on a wire rack to cool completely. They'll crisp up further when cool.

6. Use your imagination to decorate the butterflies using the glitter pens, glitter and sprinkles – have lots of glittery fun!

Rainbow Magic cookies

Spirals of rainbow-coloured dough make magical-looking biscuits –
these are a perfect present for friends and family.

Makes: 12

Preparation: 45 minutes,
plus chilling

Bake: 20 minutes

You will need:

+ 125g unsalted butter,
  softened, cut into pieces

+ 80g caster sugar

+ 1 teaspoon vanilla extract

+ 1 large egg yolk

+ 200g plain flour, plus extra
  for dusting

+ ½ teaspoon baking powder

+ Red, orange, yellow, green,
  blue gel food colouring

Special equipment:

+ 2 large baking trays

+ Baking paper

Top Tip!
These biscuits are
delicious plain –
or stir in chocolate
chips.

1. Line two baking trays with baking paper. Heat the oven to
180C/160C fan/Gas 4.

2. Using an electric hand whisk, beat together the butter and
sugar in a large mixing bowl until pale and fluffy – this will take
about 5 minutes. Add the vanilla extract and egg yolk and whisk
again on a low speed.

3. Sift in the flour and baking powder, then mix in with a wooden
spoon to make a smooth dough. Wrap the dough in cling film
and chill for 30 minutes to firm up.

4. Now it's time to colour the dough! Divide the dough into five
pieces, about 80g each. Flatten one piece of dough on a worktop
and add a large pea-sized amount of red colouring. Gently knead
the dough until it is an even red colour, adding more colour if
needed. Repeat with the orange, yellow, green and blue gel food
colouring to make five rainbow-coloured pieces of dough.

5. Lightly flour the work surface and rolling pin. Roll out the red
dough into a long rectangle, about 6cm wide.

6. Roll out the orange dough to the same size as the red dough
and place it on top. Repeat with the yellow, green and blue
dough, so you have a rainbow-coloured stack of dough. Cut the
dough in half horizontally so that you end up with two smaller
rectangles of multi-coloured dough.

7. Tightly roll up one half of the dough from the short side into a
cylinder, then cut into six 1cm thick rounds. Repeat with the second half of dough. Using the palm of your hand, press each piece
of dough into a round biscuit shape, about 5mm thick.

8. Arrange the dough on the baking trays, placed slightly apart.
Bake for 15 to 20 minutes until slightly crisp. Leave to cool for
5 minutes on the trays, then place on a wire rack to cool and
crisp up further.

⁺Magical meringues⁺

Swirly whirly meringue kisses taste as good as they look. Enjoy them plain or sandwich together with fluffy whipped vanilla cream.

Makes: about 28
Preparation: 25 minutes
Bake: 1½ hours, plus cooling

You will need:

✦ 2 large egg whites, at room temperature

✦ 125g white caster sugar

✦ Light pink, light blue and orange gel food colouring

Cream Filling (optional):

✦ 120g double cream

✦ 1 tablespoon icing sugar

✦ ½ teaspoon vanilla extract

Special equipment:

✦ 2 large baking trays

✦ Piping bag with medium open star nozzle

✦ Baking paper

Top Tip!
No piping bag? Place spoonfuls of the meringue mix on the baking trays instead.

1. Heat the oven to 140C/120C fan/Gas 1. Using a 3cm glass or plain cutter as a template, draw 14 circles on a sheet of baking paper, spaced slightly apart. The paper should be the same size as your baking tray. Repeat with a second sheet of baking paper and baking tray. Turn the paper over so the drawn circles are on the underneath – you can fix it in place with blobs of meringue.

2. Using an electric hand whisk, whisk the egg whites in a large, grease-free mixing bowl until it's doubled in size with soft peaks.

3. Whisking continuously, gradually add the sugar – one tablespoon at a time – until you have a thick, glossy meringue mixture with stiff peaks. The meringue should hold its shape when you lift the whisk.

4. For the swirly coloured meringue, fit your piping bag with the nozzle and fold down the top. Stand the bag upright in a glass – this will make it easier to spoon in the meringue mixture. Brush a stripe of each food colour inside the length of the piping bag, working from the nozzle upwards.

5. Using a metal spoon, spoon the meringue into the bag, then twist the top and squeeze the mixture down towards the nozzle. Using the rounds on the baking paper as a guide, hold the piping bag vertical to the baking tray. Gently squeeze to pipe a swirl of meringue, working from the middle out and quickly drawing up the piping bag to make a peak. Bake the meringues for 1¼–1½ hours until crisp on the outside. Turn off the oven and leave the meringues to cool in the oven with the door ajar.

6. If using, make the cream filling. Using an electric hand whisk, whip the cream, sugar and vanilla extract (you could colour the cream using food colouring) to fluffy firm peaks. Place a spoonful of the cream mixture on one cooled meringue and sandwich with a second meringue. Alternatively, serve the meringues plain.

Marshmallow Fairy treats

These magical squares of pink, glittery marshmallow cake are so quick and easy to make –
they're ready in a wave of a fairy wand!

Makes: about 20
Preparation: 10 minutes
Cook: 5 minutes

You will need:

+ 50g unsalted butter, plus extra for greasing

+ 300g mini pink and white marshmallows

+ 175g rice pop cereal

+ 2 tablespoons sprinkles

To decorate:

+ Edible glitter, to decorate

Special equipment:

+ 23cm square baking tin

1. Grease the bottom and sides of a 23cm square baking tin.

2. Gently melt the butter in a large saucepan. Add the marshmallows and, using a wooden spoon, stir until melted. Take the pan off the heat.

3. Using a metal spoon, stir in the rice pop cereal and sprinkles until everything is mixed together.

4. Spoon the mixture into the greased tin and press into an even layer with the back of the spoon – it is very sticky, so it helps if the spoon is slightly wet. When the top is flat, sprinkle with edible glitter and/or more sprinkles. Leave to cool and firm up, then cut into 20 squares.

Top Tip!
Use your favourite sprinkles to decorate these marshmallow squares.

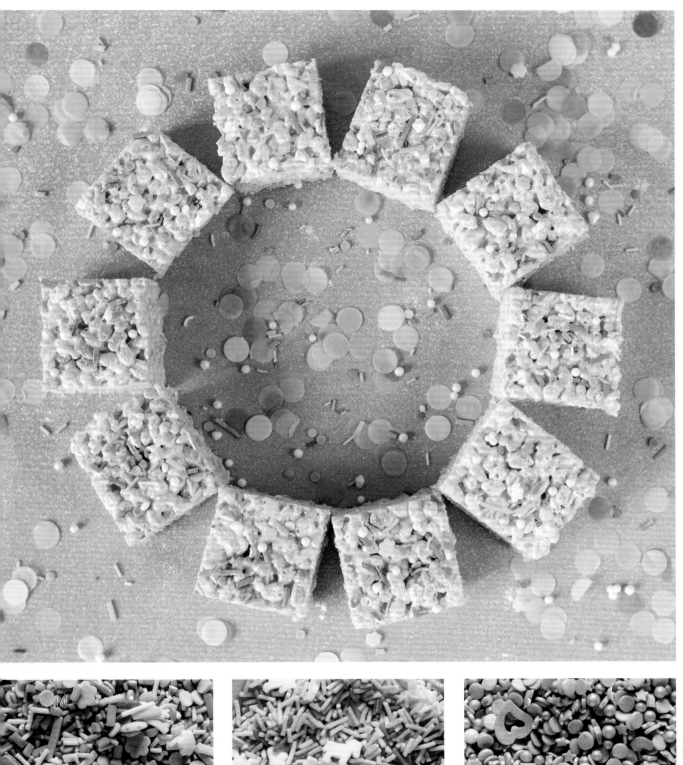

✦ Fairy pillows ✦

Light and airy just like fairy pillows… These cheese puffs are just the thing for parties, or make a delicious snack!

Makes: about 17
Preparation: 30 minutes,
Bake: 25 minutes

You will need:

✦ 125ml water

✦ 40g unsalted butter, cut into small pieces

✦ ¼ teaspoon salt

✦ 75g plain flour

✦ 2 large eggs, beaten

✦ 85g mature Cheddar cheese, finely grated

Special equipment:

✦ 2 large baking trays

✦ Baking paper

Top Tip!
Dip the cheese puffs into tomato sauce or hummus for a tasty snack.

1. Heat the oven to 220C/200C fan/Gas 7 and line two baking trays with baking paper.

2. Heat the water, butter and salt in a medium saucepan over a medium heat, stirring twice. When it starts to bubble, stir, then remove the pan from the heat.

3. Using a balloon whisk, mix in half the flour, then add the rest of the flour. Mix first with the whisk and then a wooden spoon when the mixture becomes too thick – it should be a smooth paste the same consistency as mashed potato.

4. Put the pan back on a medium-low heat and cook, beating continuously with the wooden spoon, for 5 minutes until a smooth, dark cream-coloured paste. It should come away from the sides of the pan into a ball. (There may also be a slight film of mixture on the bottom of the pan.)

5. Put the mixture into the bowl of a stand mixer fitted with the paddle attachment, or use an electric hand whisk, and beat the dough for 3 minutes to let it cool slightly. Add a third of the egg and beat until mixed in, then repeat twice more with the rest of the egg. Stir in the cheese. The mixture should now look thick, smooth and glossy.

6. Using a tablespoon, place heaped rounds of the mixture onto the baking trays, spacing them well apart. You will have enough mixture for about 17 Fairy Pillows. Gently flatten any peaks with a damp finger.

7. Put the trays in the oven for 5 minutes. Turn the heat down to 180C/160C fan/Gas 4 and bake for another 15 minutes until risen and light golden. Carefully pierce each one with a cocktail stick to release any steam, then return to the oven for another 5 minutes until golden and puffed up – just like fairy pillows! Leave to cool for 5 minutes on the trays, then place on a wire rack to cool further.

Magical
breads & pastries

✦Rainbow✦ rolls

Cut these soft, fluffy rolls in half to discover the colours of the rainbow – they're delicious with sweet or savoury fillings.

Makes: 8
Preparation: 1 hour, plus rising
Bake: 30 minutes

You will need:

✦ 400g strong bread flour, plus extra for dusting

✦ 7g dried instant yeast

✦ 1 teaspoon sugar

✦ 1 rounded teaspoon salt

✦ 160ml lukewarm whole milk

✦ 100ml lukewarm water

✦ 1 egg, lightly beaten

✦ Blue, green, yellow, orange and red gel food colouring

✦ Light oil, for greasing

Special equipment:

✦ 2 small pans

✦ 2 large baking trays

Top Tip!
Yeast likes lukewarm water – too hot and it will not help the dough rise.

1. Put the flour in the bowl of a stand mixer fitted with a dough hook, or a large mixing bowl, then add the yeast and sugar to one side and the salt to the other side. Mix together the flour mixture.

2. Gently heat the water and milk in seperate pans on your hob, but do not boil. Stir in the lukewarm milk, lukewarm water and egg into the flour mixture. Knead the dough in the stand mixer for 5 minutes. Alternatively, turn the ball of dough out onto a lightly floured work surface and knead for 10 minutes until the dough is smooth and springs back when you press it with your fingers.

3. Divide the dough into five balls. Press one ball out slightly and add three pea-sized blobs of blue gel colouring. Knead the dough until the colour is evenly mixed in, then set aside, covered, in a lightly oiled bowl. Repeat with each ball of dough until you have five bright rainbow-coloured balls in blue, green, yellow, orange and red. Place each one in a separate oiled bowl, cover, and leave to rise for 1 hour or until doubled in size.

4. When the dough has risen, roll out each ball into a 20cm x 16cm rectangle. Place the blue rectangle of dough on the bottom and top with the green, yellow, orange and red rectangles of dough to make a stack with five layers.

5. Cut the dough into eight 2cm-wide long strips. Take one end of a strip in each hand and twist in opposite directions to make a multi-coloured rope. Form the rope into a ring, then press and twist the ends together to seal. Place on a lined baking tray and repeat with the rest of the dough strips to make eight rolls in total.

6. Cover the trays with clean tea towels and leave to rest for 30 minutes to prove – they should be about a third larger when ready.

7. Meanwhile, heat the oven to 200C/180C fan/Gas 6. Bake the rolls for 25 minutes, turning over halfway, or until they sound hollow when tapped underneath. Leave to cool on a wire rack.

Fluffy Unicorn buns

Top these sweet, fluffy buns with colourful fondant unicorn horns – see how to make the horns on page 5, then leave to harden while the buns rise.

Makes: 6
Preparation: 45 minutes, plus rising
Bake: 15 minutes

You will need:

+ 275g strong bread flour
+ 7g instant dried yeast
+ 25g caster sugar
+ ¼ teaspoon salt
+ 20g unsalted butter, softened, cut into small pieces
+ 175ml lukewarm whole milk, plus extra for glazing
+ Oil, for greasing

Cream filling:

+ 175g double cream
+ 2 tablespoons icing sugar, plus extra for dusting
+ ½ teaspoon vanilla extract
+ Orange, pink and yellow gel food colouring
+ 6 heaped teaspoons strawberry jam

To decorate:

+ Edible black writing pen or icing

Special equipment:

+ 1 large baking tray
+ Piping bag with a medium closed star nozzle

1. Put the flour in the bowl of a stand mixer fitted with a dough hook, or a large mixing bowl, then add the yeast and sugar to one side and the salt to the other side.

2. Mix the flour mixture together, then stir in the butter and lukewarm milk. Knead the dough in the stand mixer for 5 minutes. Alternatively, turn the ball of dough out onto a lightly floured work surface and knead for 10 minutes until smooth and it springs back when pressed with your fingers. Place the dough in an oiled bowl and leave to rise for 1½ hours or until doubled in size.

3. Weigh the dough and divide into six pieces, then shape each one into a ball with the seam underneath. Arrange the dough balls on a lined baking tray, making sure they are spaced well apart. Cover with a clean tea towel and leave to rise for 45 minutes or until doubled in size.

4. Heat the oven to 190C/170C fan/Gas 5. Brush the top of each bun with milk and bake for 15 minutes or until risen and fluffy and the underside sounds hollow when tapped. Transfer to a wire rack to cool.

5. To make the filling, whip the cream, icing sugar and vanilla extract to soft, fluffy peaks. To make stripy-coloured cream, paint three different-coloured stripes – pink, yellow and orange – down the length of the piping bag, evenly spaced apart. Spoon the cream into the piping bag, twist the top to seal.

6. Using a knife, cut a deep, long slit along the top of each bun. Spoon the jam into the bottom of each split – ask someone to help you hold the buns open to make them easier to fill. Holding the piping bag upright, pipe a generous swirl of stripy-coloured cream down the length of each bun.

7. To make the eyes, pipe or draw two black unicorn eyes on one end of each bun. (You could also top with a fondant horn, see page 5.) Dust each bun with a little icing sugar, if liked.

Unicorn Plaited bread

Strands of pink, purple and orange dough look like the flowing mane of a unicorn when plaited together – they also make a yummy loaf!

Makes: 1 loaf
Preparation: 25 minutes, plus rising
Bake: 40 minutes

You will need:

+ 260ml lukewarm water

+ 7g dried instant yeast

+ 2 teaspoons caster sugar

+ 400g strong bread flour, plus extra for dusting

+ 25g unsalted butter, chilled, cut into small pieces

+ 1 rounded teaspoon salt

+ Pink, orange, purple gel food colouring

+ oil, for greasing

Special equipment:

+ 1 large baking tray

Top Tip!
The bread can also be cooked in a loaf tin – choose a 900g one.

1. Mix together the warm water, yeast and sugar in a small bowl, then set aside.

2. Put the flour in the bowl of a stand mixer fitted with a dough hook, or a large mixing bowl. Add the butter and rub it in with your fingertips to make rough crumbs. Stir in the salt.

3. Stir in the yeast water and mix until combined to a rough dough. Knead the dough in the stand mixer for 5 minutes. Alternatively, turn the dough out onto a lightly floured work surface and knead for 10 minutes until smooth and it springs back when pressed.

4. Divide the dough into three balls, about 230g each. Now it's time to colour the dough! Press one ball of dough out slightly, add two pea-sized blobs of pink colouring and knead for 5 minutes until an even pink colour. Set aside in a lightly oiled bowl, covered with a clean tea towel.

5. Repeat with the orange and purple colouring until you have three coloured balls of dough. Place each one in a separate oiled bowl, cover and leave to rise for 1 hour or until doubled in size.

6. When the dough has risen, roll out each ball into a 30cm x 5cm-long sausage on a lightly floured work surface. Place the three long strips of dough together on a lightly floured baking tray with the orange one in the middle. Press the dough together at one end to join, then plait the dough and tuck the opposite end under to seal. Cover the tray with a clean tea towel and leave to prove for 30 minutes – it should have almost doubled in size when ready.

7. Meanwhile, heat the oven to 200C/180C fan/Gas 6. Bake the bread for 35 to 40 minutes until risen and the loaf sounds hollow when tapped underneath. Leave to cool on a wire rack.

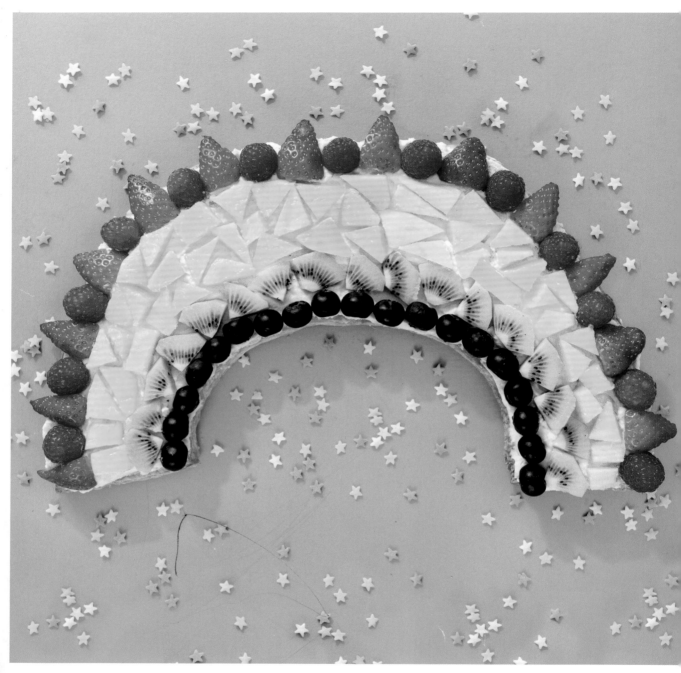

⋆·Rainbow Fruit pizza·⋆

Everyone loves rainbows ... and this fruit-topped rainbow pizza is fun to make.
Choose your favourite fruit to make the rainbow topping – the more colourful the better!

Makes: 1 (serves about 8)
Preparation: 30 minutes
Bake: 20 minutes

You will need:

✦ 320g ready-rolled all-butter puff pastry, about 35cm x 25cm

✦ 240ml double cream

✦ 1 tsp vanilla extract

✦ 2 tablespoons icing sugar, plus extra for dusting

To decorate:

✦ Blueberries, about 200g

✦ 2 kiwi fruit, peeled, quartered and sliced

✦ Mango, cut into small pieces, about 250g

✦ Strawberries, halved or quartered if large, about 200g

✦ Raspberries, about 125g

Special equipment:

✦ 2 large rectangular baking sheets

✦ Baking paper

Top Tip!
Grapes, pineapple, blackberries, apple, plums and peaches are tasty too!

1. Heat the oven to 220C/200C fan/Gas 6. Lightly dust a sheet of baking paper the same size as your baking sheet with a little icing sugar.

2. Roll out the pastry a little, until about 2–3mm thick, and carefully place on the baking paper.

3. Cut the pastry into a rainbow shape, using as much of the pastry as possible. You could do this freehand or make a cardboard template. Using a side plate as a template, cut a semi-circular rainbow-shape from the middle.

4. Slide the rainbow-shaped pastry on the paper onto the baking sheet and sprinkle the top with icing sugar. Top with a second sheet of baking paper and place the second baking sheet on top. This will help to keep the pastry flat when it bakes.

5. Bake the pastry rainbow for 10 minutes, then carefully remove the top baking tray and paper. Put the pastry back in the oven for another 5 to 10 minutes until light golden and cooked through. Leave to cool on the sheet, pressing the pastry down a little to flatten if it has risen in places.

6. Meanwhile, make the whipped cream topping. Whisk together the double cream, vanilla extract and icing sugar to soft peaks.

7. To decorate the rainbow, spread the whipped cream mixture over the pastry, leaving a narrow border around the edge. Arrange the blueberries, kiwi, mango, strawberries and raspberries on top in rainbow stripes.

Sparkly, Snowy cinnamon buns

These pretty, sparkly, iced cinnamon buns are easy to prepare
and make a delicious teatime treat!

Makes: about 12
Preparation: 20 minutes,
plus chilling
Bake: 20 minutes

You will need:

✦ 35g unsalted butter, plus
   extra for greasing

✦ 70g light soft brown sugar

✦ 1 tablespoon ground
   cinnamon

✦ 375g ready-rolled puff
   pastry

Lemon icing:

✦ 3 tablespoons icing sugar

✦ 2 teaspoons lemon juice

To decorate:

✦ Blue, white and violet
   sprinkles

Special equipment:

✦ 20cm shallow round
   baking tin

Top Tip!
The icing is
flavoured with
lemon, but you could
use orange.

1. Line the base and grease the sides of the baking tin. Melt the butter in a small pan over a low heat. Remove from the heat and leave to cool for 2 minutes.

2. Mix together the brown sugar and cinnamon in a bowl.

3. Unroll the pastry, with the long edge facing you, then brush all over with the melted butter. Scatter the sugar and cinnamon mixture over the top in an even layer.

4. Working from the long edge, tightly roll up the pastry into a long cylinder. Trim each end to neaten, then cut the pastry into 12 3cm-wide rounds.

5. Press the edge of each bun to seal and neaten the shape into a round, then arrange in the tin. Arrange nine buns around the edge of the tin, spaced about 1cm apart so they have room to spread. Place the remaining three buns in the middle, then chill for 30 minutes.

6. Heat the oven to 220C/200C fan/Gas 7. Bake for 20 minutes or until the pastry is cooked and the buns are risen and golden. Leave in the tin or turn out after 5 minutes.

7. While the buns are baking, make the icing. Sift the icing sugar into a bowl and stir in the lemon juice until smooth and thick enough to coat the back of a spoon. Drizzle the icing over the buns, then scatter with the sprinkles.

Sunbeam Fairy tarts

These special lemon tarts are topped with a swirl of meringue
that is bursting with happy sunshine colours.

Makes: about 12
Preparation: 40 minutes,
plus chilling
Bake: 35 minutes

You will need:

✦ Unsalted butter, for
   greasing

✦ 375g ready-made
   shortcrust pastry

✦ Flour, for dusting

✦ 12 tablespoons lemon curd

✦ 1 egg white

✦ 55g caster sugar

✦ ½ teaspoon cornflour

✦ Yellow and orange gel
   food colouring

Special equipment:

✦ 12-hole fairy cake tin

✦ 6.5cm fluted pastry cutter

✦ Piping bag with large open
   star nozzle

Top Tip!
Place large
spoonfuls of yellow
and orange-coloured
meringue on top of
each tart instead
of piping.

1. Lightly grease the holes of a fairy cake tin with butter.

2. Unroll the pastry on a lightly floured worktop. Using the 6.5cm pastry cutter, cut out 12 pastry rounds. Carefully press the pastry rounds into the fairy cake tin, then chill for 20 minutes.

3. Heat the oven to 200C/180C fan/Gas 6. While the oven is heating, spoon the lemon curd into the pastry cases. Bake for 15 to 20 minutes until the pastry is crisp and light golden. Leave the tarts to cool.

4. Meanwhile, make the meringue. Whisk the egg white in a stand mixer, or using an electric hand whisk, to soft peaks. Gradually, add the sugar, one tablespoon at a time, whisking continuously to stiff, shiny peaks. Gently fold in the cornflour with a metal spoon.

5. Turn the oven down to 170C/150C fan/Gas 3.

6. Brush a thin stripe of yellow food colouring down the inside of the piping bag, starting from the nozzle end to halfway up the bag. Repeat on the opposite side of the bag with a thin stripe of orange colouring.

7. Spoon the meringue into the bag and twist the top to seal, then squeeze the meringue down to the nozzle. Pipe a swirl of meringue on top of each tart into a large peak. Bake for 10 to 15 minutes until the meringue starts to colour and turn crisp. Enjoy warm or cold!

35

✦ ⋆ Unicorn ⋆ Horns ⋆

These golden pastry cones look similar to unicorn horns! They're filled with a yummy strawberry cream.

Makes: 6
Preparation: 40 minutes, plus chilling
Bake: 30 minutes

You will need:

+ sunflower oil, for greasing

+ 160g ready-rolled puff pastry

+ 1 egg, lightly beaten

+ 2 tablespoons demerara sugar

Cream filling:

+ 100g strawberries

+ 100g double cream

+ 2 teaspoons icing sugar, plus extra for dusting

+ ½ teaspoon vanilla extract

Pink icing:

+ 3 tablespoons icing sugar

+ 2 teaspoons lemon juice

+ Few drops pink gel food colouring

Special equipment:

+ 1 large baking tray

+ 6 metal cone moulds, about 10cm long

+ Piping bag with small star nozzle

+ Baking paper

1. Heat the oven 200C/180C fan/Gas 6 and line the baking tray with baking paper. Lightly grease the metal cones with oil.

2. Roll out the puff pastry a little, then cut into six 1cm-wide long strips.

3. Starting at the tip of the metal cone, wrap a strip of pastry around, slightly overlapping it as you work your way up – it should look like a unicorn horn! Leave a 3cm gap at the top to make it easier to remove the cone after baking. Place the pastry-wrapped cone on the baking tray, then repeat to make six in total. Chill for 15 minutes.

4. Just before baking, brush the cones with egg and sprinkle over the demerara sugar. Bake for 25 to 30 minutes until golden and crisp, then leave to cool on the baking tray. When cold, carefully remove the metal cones from the pastry.

5. Meanwhile make the filling, blend the strawberries to a purée, then set aside. Using a hand electric whisk, whip the cream, icing sugar and vanilla extract to soft peaks. Stir in the strawberry purée and chill until needed.

6. To make the pink icing, sift the icing sugar into a bowl and stir in the lemon juice until smooth and thick enough to coat the back of a spoon. Stir in a few drops of pink colouring.

7. Spoon the cream filling into the piping bag fitted with the nozzle. Pipe the cream into each cone – it helps if someone holds the cone upright for you. Using a teaspoon, drizzle over a little pink icing and leave to set.

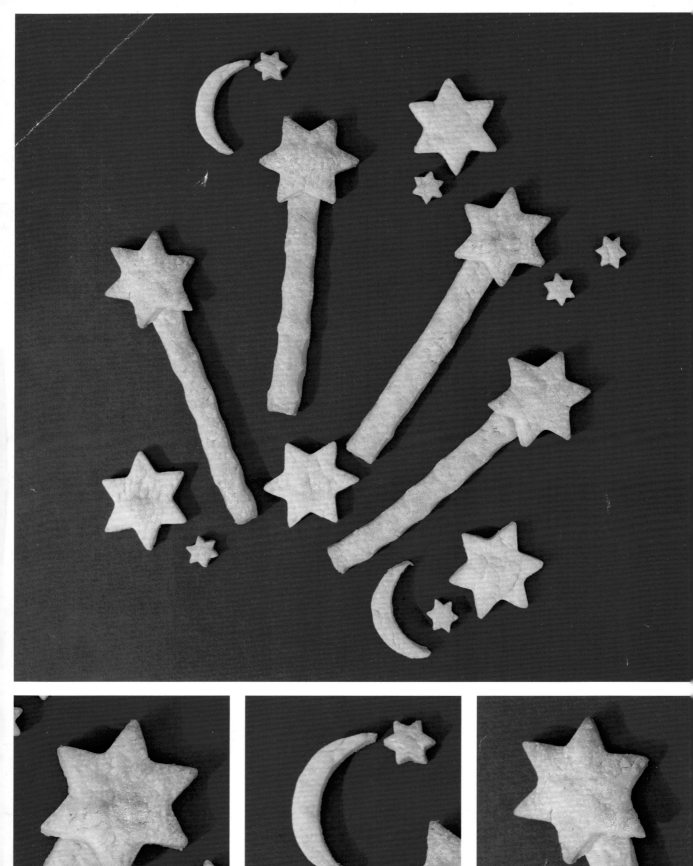

Fairy wands

Make magical things happen with a wave of a wand – they taste magic too!

Makes: 8, plus extra stars
Preparation: 30 minutes
Bake: 12 minutes

You will need:

✦ 150g plain flour, sifted, plus extra for dusting

✦ ¼ teaspoon salt

✦ 90g unsalted butter, chilled, cut into small pieces

✦ 50g parmesan cheese, finely grated

✦ 2 egg yolks

✦ 1 teaspoon milk, plus extra for brushing

To decorate:

✦ Edible gold powder (optional)

Special equipment:

✦ 2 baking trays

✦ Baking paper

✦ Medium star cutter, small star cutter and moon cutter

Top Tip!
Swap cheddar cheese for the parmesan — it's just as delicious!

1. Heat the oven to 200C/180C fan/Gas 6 and line two baking trays with baking paper.

2. Mix together the flour and salt in a large mixing bowl. Rub in the butter with your fingertips to make rough crumbs, then stir in the parmesan cheese.

3. Using a fork, mix in the egg yolks and milk, then bring the mixture together with your hands to make a ball of dough.

4. Lightly flour a work surface. Roll out the dough with a rolling pin into a rectangle, about 5mm thick. Using the star cutter, stamp out eight stars. Cut out eight wands, about 16cm long x 2cm wide.

5. Brush a little milk over the middle of the back of one pastry star. Press a wand on top and flatten the top edge to attach the star to the wand. Carefully turn it over and place on a baking tray. Repeat to make eight wands in total. Roll out any spare pastry and cut out extra stars and moons.

6. Bake for 10 to 12 minutes until light golden and crisp. Leave to cool for 10 minutes, then transfer to a wire rack to cool completely. To decorate, brush each star with a little edible gold powder to give it a sparkly finish, if you like.

Hidden Treasure parcels

Take a bite to discover what's inside these little savoury, crispy filo pastry parcels!

Makes: 28
Preparation: 1 hour
Bake: 25 minutes

You will need:

+ 6 reduced-fat sausages, about 350g

+ 1 eating apple

+ 1 tablespoon grainy mustard

+ 70g fresh breadcrumbs

+ 65g unsalted butter

+ 7 sheets filo pastry, 270g pack

+ Salt and freshly ground black pepper

+ 28 long chives, to decorate (optional)

Special equipment:

+ 2 large baking trays

Top Tip!
Make sure you use low-fat sausages as they stop the pastry turning soggy.

1. To make the filling, squeeze the sausages out of their skins into a large mixing bowl. (Wash your hands thoroughly afterwards.)

2. Grate the whole apple, no need to peel it first, using the large holes of a box grater, discarding the core. Add the grated apple to the sausage meat with the mustard and breadcrumbs. Season with a little salt and pepper, then mix everything together.

3. Melt the butter in a small pan and remove from the heat. Heat the oven to 180C/160C fan/Gas 4.

4. To make the parcels, place a filo sheet on the work top with the long edge facing towards you and cut into eight equal-sized pieces. First, cut the filo sheet into quarters, then cut each quarter in half vertically. Repeat with the rest of the filo sheets. Cover with a damp, clean tea towel to stop them drying out until ready to use. Take two pieces of filo, keeping the rest covered. Lightly brush one of the sheets with butter, then top with the second sheet.

5. Place a heaped teaspoon of the filling mixture in the centre of the filo in a pile. Brush a little more butter around the filling. Gather up the pastry around the filling and pinch together tightly at the top to secure. Flare out the top of the filo into a 'moneybag' shape. Lightly brush with butter and place on the baking tray. Repeat to make 28 small parcels in total.

6. Bake the parcels for 20 to 25 minutes or until cooked through and golden all over – watch the tops don't brown too much. Any leftover filling mixture can be rolled into balls and cooked alongside the parcels. Tie a chive around each parcel, if liked, and serve warm or at room temperature.

Magical Cakes
(big and small)

✦ *Make-a-wish* cakes ✦

Your very own special, lucky rainbow cakes – blow out the candle and make a wish!

Makes: 7
Preparation: 45 minutes
Bake: 40 minutes

You will need:

✦ 200g unsalted butter, softened

✦ 200g caster sugar

✦ 3 large eggs, lightly beaten

✦ 1 teaspoon vanilla extract

✦ 200g self-raising flour, sifted

✦ 1 teaspoon baking powder, sifted

✦ 3 tablespoons whole milk

✦ ½ recipe quantity Vanilla Buttercream (see page 4)

To decorate:

✦ Red, orange, yellow, green, blue gel food colouring

✦ Rainbow sprinkles

✦ Coloured candles

Special equipment:

✦ 23cm round cake tin

✦ 6cm diameter deep round cutter

✦ Piping bag with a large closed star nozzle

✦ Baking paper

1. Heat the oven to 180C/160C fan/Gas 4. Line a 23cm round tin with baking paper and grease the sides.

2. To make the cake, beat the butter and caster sugar in the bowl of a stand mixer, or using an electric hand whisk, for 3 to 5 minutes until pale, creamy and fluffy. You will have to scrape down the sides of the bowl from time to time.

3. Add the eggs, a little at a time, beating well, then the vanilla extract and beat again. Add the flour, baking powder and then the milk to the bowl and fold in gently until smooth and creamy.

4. To make the rainbow colours, divide the cake mixture between five bowls, about 150g each. Add a large pea-sized quantity of red food colouring and gently mix in with a cocktail stick, then with a spatula to make a red cake mixture. Add more of the colour if you need to. Repeat with the orange, yellow, green and blue food colouring to make five rainbow-coloured bowls of cake mixture.

5. Place large spoonfuls of the different-coloured cake mixture into the tin. Using a palette knife, spread out the mixture to an even layer without mixing the colours too much. Tap the tin lightly on a work surface to get rid of any air bubbles.

6. Bake for 35 to 40 minutes until risen, golden and a skewer inserted into the middle comes out clean. Leave in the tin for 5 minutes, then turn out onto a wire rack to cool completely. When the cake is cool, stamp out seven cakes using the 6cm deep round cutter. Save any spare sponge to make the Unicorn Cake Pops on page 9.

7. Make the buttercream following the instructions on page 4. Spoon the buttercream into a piping bag fitted with the nozzle. Twist the end to seal and squeeze the buttercream down to the nozzle. Pipe a large swirl of buttercream on top of each cake, working from the outer edge to the middle in a circular motion, draw up the piping bag sharply to make a peak.

8. Place a birthday candle in the middle of each cake and scatter over a few rainbow sprinkles. Don't forget to make a wish!

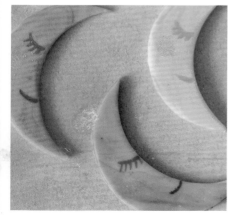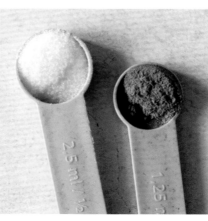

Over-the-moon Muffins

Have a go at creating your own magical moon and star decorations to top these banana muffins. It's best to make them a few hours – or a day – in advance to let them harden before placing on top of the cakes.

Makes: 12
Preparation: 1 hour, plus drying
Bake: 30 minutes

You will need:

+ 3 very ripe bananas, peeled (about 320g peeled weight)

+ 250g self-raising flour, sifted

+ ½ teaspoon salt

+ 150g caster sugar

+ ½ teaspoon ground cinnamon

+ 100g unsalted butter, cut into pieces

+ 2 medium eggs, lightly beaten

To decorate:

+ About 120g white fondant icing

+ Blue, orange, pink gel food colouring

+ Edible coloured pens

+ Icing sugar, for dusting

+ ½ recipe quantity vanilla buttercream (see page 4)

Special equipment:

+ 12-hole deep muffin tin

+ 12 deep muffin cases

1. First make the fondant moon and star decorations. Add a few drops of blue, orange or pink food colouring and lightly knead into the fondant. (Alternatively, leave plain and decorate the cut-out shapes using edible colouring pens and glitter.) Sprinkle a little icing sugar over the worktop and roll out the fondant until about 3–4mm thick. Cut out your chosen shapes using a cutter or upturned glass, then decorate with a face, star or pattern. Let them dry and harden for a few hours, or overnight.

2. Heat the oven to 180C/160C fan/Gas 4 and place the muffin cases in the muffin tin.

3. Mash the bananas in a bowl until smooth, then leave to one side. Mix together the flour, salt, sugar and cinnamon in a large mixing bowl with a wooden spoon.

4. Melt the butter in a small pan over a low heat and leave to cool for a couple of minutes. Using a wooden spoon, mix the melted butter, eggs and mashed bananas into the flour mixture until everything is combined.

5. Spoon the mixture into the muffin cases, then bake for 25 to 30 minutes until risen and a skewer inserted into the middle comes out clean. Leave to cool on a wire rack.

6. Meanwhile, make the buttercream following the instructions on page 4. Spoon or pipe a swirl of buttercream on top of each muffin and top with the moon and star decorations. (You could try cutting your icing into your own favourite shapes – rainbows, flowers, hearts.)

✦ Rosebud fairy cakes ✦

Flower fairies love these pretty cakes with their swirl of rose-coloured buttercream.

Makes: 12
Preparation: 30 minutes
Bake: 20 minutes

You will need:

✦ 150g unsalted butter, softened, cut into pieces

✦ 150g caster sugar

✦ 2 large eggs, lightly beaten

✦ 150g self-raising flour, sifted

✦ ½ teaspoon baking powder

✦ 2 tablespoons whole milk

✦ 1 teaspoon vanilla extract

To decorate:

✦ Vanilla buttercream (see page 4)

✦ Dried strawberry pieces

✦ Rainbow chocolate buttons

Special equipment:

✦ 12-hole fairy tin

✦ 12 pink fairy cases

✦ Piping bag with medium open star nozzle

Top Tip!
No piping bag? Spoon a large dollop of the pink and white buttercream on top of each cake instead.

1. Heat the oven to 180C/160C fan/Gas 4 and place the cupcake cases in the fairy tin.

2. Beat the butter and sugar in the bowl of a stand mixer, or using an electric hand whisk, for 3 to 5 minutes until pale, creamy and fluffy. Add the eggs, one at a time, beating well. Add the flour and baking powder, then the milk and vanilla extract and fold in gently until smooth and creamy.

3. Spoon the cake mixture into the cupcake cases, then bake for 15 to 20 minutes until risen and a skewer inserted into the middle comes out clean. Leave to cool on a wire rack.

4. Meanwhile, make the buttercream following the instructions on page 4. Divide the buttercream between two bowls. Add a few drops of pink food colouring to one bowl to make a dark pink icing and stir gently to blend in. Leave the buttercream in the second bowl plain.

5. Lay a rectangular piece of cling film on the worktop. Spoon the pink and plain buttercream in two long horizontal 'sausages' next to each other on the cling film. Taking the bottom edge of the cling film, carefully roll up the icing into a long, stripy cylinder. Fold the cling film over at one end to seal and place the open end in a piping bag fitted with the nozzle.

6. Pipe a large swirl of buttercream on top of each cupcake, working from the middle to the outer edge in a circular motion and back to the centre, draw up the piping bag sharply to make a peak.

7. Sprinkle with dried strawberry pieces and finish each cake with two rainbow button fairy wings.

✦✦Baby Unicorn cakes✦✦

Your very own baby unicorn cakes – they're super cute! Why not have fun choosing a unicorn name and decorating each one with a different coloured horn and sprinkles?

Makes: 5
Preparation: 2 hours
Bake: 25 minutes

You will need:

✦ Vanilla Sponge (see page 48)

✦ 5 heaped teaspoons strawberry jam

✦ Vanilla buttercream (see page 4)

To decorate:

✦ 100g white fondant icing

✦ Edible gold powder

✦ Violet, pink and yellow gel food colouring

✦ 30g black fondant or edible black writing icing

✦ Coloured sprinkles

Special equipment:

✦ 5 x 6cm wide x 5cm deep, flat-bottomed dariole moulds

✦ Cake scraper

✦ Piping bag with small closed star nozzle

Top Tip!
See page 5 for how to make unicorn horns, ears and eyes.

1. First make ten unicorn ears and five horns using the white fondant, edible gold powder and food colouring, then five pairs of eyes with the black fondant following the instructions on page 5. Leave them to harden overnight or for a few hours.

2. Heat the oven to 200C/180C fan/Gas 6 and lightly grease the dariole moulds with butter.

3. Make the cakes following steps 2–3 for the Rosebud Fairy Cakes (see page 48). Divide the cake mixture equally between the dariole moulds. Bake for 20 to 25 minutes or until risen, golden and a skewer inserted into the middle comes out clean. Leave the cakes in the moulds for 5 minutes, then turn out to cool completely on a wire rack.

4. Slice the cakes in half horizontally. Spread a heaped teaspoon of strawberry jam over the bottom half of each sponge, then top with the second half.

5. Meanwhile, make the buttercream (see page 4). Spread a layer of white buttercream over the top and down the sides of each cake using a palette knife. Smooth with a cake scraper or palette knife and repeat to cover five cakes.

6. To decorate, scatter sprinkles around the bottom of each cake. Place a unicorn horn on top – the buttercream should hold it in place – then place an ear either side of the horn. Place two eyes on the front of each cake, or draw the eyes directly onto the cakes with black writing icing.

7. For the unicorn mane, paint three large dots of each food colouring – violet, pink and yellow – on the inside of the piping bag fitted with the nozzle. Fill with the remaining buttercream, twist the end to seal, then squeeze the buttercream towards the nozzle. Pipe small rosettes of buttercream on the top of each cake to make multi-coloured unicorn mane. Enjoy!

Gold-dust brownies

The best brownies have a soft, squidgy, gooey centre and these are extra special with a caramel sauce drizzle and sparkly gold decorations. A gold star goes to the baker!

Makes: 12
Preparation: 20 minutes, plus cooling
Bake: 25 minutes

You will need:

✦ 200g unsalted butter, cut into small pieces, plus extra for greasing

✦ 50g plain chocolate, broken into even-sized chunks

✦ 250g golden caster sugar

✦ 3 medium eggs, lightly beaten

✦ 115g plain flour, sifted

✦ Pinch of salt

✦ 55g cocoa powder, sifted

To decorate:

✦ 100g salted caramel sauce, warmed if needed

✦ Gold stars

✦ Edible gold glitter spray

Special equipment:

✦ 20cm square baking tin

✦ Baking paper

Top Tip!
For nutty brownies, stir in 60g of your favourite chopped nuts.

1. Heat the oven to 190C/170C fan/Gas 5 and line the tin with baking paper, then grease the sides.

2. Gently melt the butter and chocolate in a medium saucepan over a low heat, stirring occasionally. Pour the mixture into a large mixing bowl.

3. Using a wooden spoon, stir in the sugar until it dissolves. Next add the eggs, flour, salt and cocoa powder and stir until everything is mixed together.

4. Pour the mixture into the lined tin and bake for 20 to 25 minutes until the top is firm but the middle is still a little soft and squidgy when a skewer is inserted into the middle. Leave to cool in the tin.

5. When cool, turn the brownie out onto a wire rack. Place a serving plate or board on top and carefully flip it over so the top is facing upwards.

6. To decorate, using a teaspoon, drizzle the salted caramel sauce over the top in ribbons, then cut into 12 squares. Scatter over the gold stars and spray with edible gold glitter spray for a sparkly finish.

Over-the-rainbow cake

The best birthday cake with a lucky rainbow drizzle and rainbow sprinkles for a double colourful celebration!

Serves: about 14
Preparation: 40 minutes, plus cooling
Bake: 50 minutes

You will need:

+ 225g unsalted butter, softened, plus extra 10g melted for greasing

+ 350g caster sugar

+ 4 large eggs, lightly beaten

+ 350g plain flour

+ 2 teaspoons baking powder

+ ½ teaspoon bicarbonate of soda

+ Large pinch of salt

+ 225g plain Greek yogurt

+ 2 teaspoons vanilla extract

Rainbow icing:

+ 200g icing sugar, sifted

+ 135–150ml double cream

+ ½ teaspoon vanilla extract

+ Red, orange, yellow, green and blue gel food colouring

+ Rainbow sprinkles

Special equipment:

+ 21cm bundt tin

+ Piping bag with small writing nozzle

1. Heat the oven to 180C/160C fan/Gas 4. Next, brush the inside of the bundt tin with melted butter until lightly coated all over.

2. Beat the butter and sugar in the large mixing bowl of a stand mixer, or use an electric hand whisk, for 3 to 5 minutes until pale, creamy and fluffy. Add the eggs, a little at a time, beating well until combined.

3. Sift together the flour, baking powder, bicarbonate of soda and salt. Mix together the yogurt and vanilla. Fold in a quarter of the flour mixture and the same of the yogurt mixture, then continue until everything is added and the mixture is smooth and creamy.

4. Spoon the cake mixture into the bundt tin, give it a little tap on the worktop to get rid of any air bubbles, then level the top with a palette knife. Bake for 45 to 50 minutes until risen, golden and a skewer inserted into the middle comes out clean. Leave the cake in the tin for 5 minutes, then turn out to cool completely on a wire rack.

5. While the cake is baking, make the icing. Whisk together the icing sugar, cream and vanilla until smooth – it should have a thick, pourable consistency, but not be too runny. Add more cream or icing sugar, if too thick or too thin. Spoon half the icing over the top of the cooled cake, letting it drizzle halfway down the sides. Leave for 1 hour or until set.

6. Divide the remaining icing between five small bowls. Add a small pea-sized amount of food colouring – red, orange, yellow, green and blue – to each bowl, then mix in, adding a little extra cream if too thick. Drizzle or pipe each rainbow colour in sections over the white icing, then finish with sprinkles.

✦ Dreamy, Creamy cHee/ecake ✦

Swirls of pretty pink whipped cream make the topping of this no-bake cheesecake look super dreamy. Take a bite and you'll be on a magical adventure!

Serves: about 10
Preparation: 40 minutes, plus chilling

You will need:

+ 280ml double cream

+ 550g full-fat cream cheese, at room temperature

+ 100g icing sugar, sifted

+ 1 teaspoon vanilla extract

+ Pink gel food colouring

For the base:

+ 110g unsalted butter, cut into small pieces, plus extra for greasing

+ 250g Digestive biscuits

+ ½ teaspoon ground cinnamon

To decorate:

+ Mini coloured chocolate beans, to decorate

Special equipment:

+ 23cm loose-bottomed cake tin

+ Baking paper

Top Tip!
Top the cheesecake with fresh fruit — strawberries, mango, banana — instead of sweets.

1. Line the base of the cake tin with baking paper and lightly grease the sides with butter.

2. To make the base, put the biscuits in a sealable food bag and bash them with the end of a rolling pin to fine crumbs. Tip them into a large mixing bowl.

3. Melt the butter in a small pan over a low heat, then pour it over the biscuit crumbs. Stir in the cinnamon until everything is mixed together. Spoon the biscuit mixture into the lined tin and spread out to an even layer, pressing it down firmly with the back of a spoon. Chill for 1 hour or until firm.

4. Meanwhile, make the cheesecake topping. Using an electric hand whisk, whip the cream in a large mixing bowl to soft peaks. Whisk the cream cheese, icing sugar and vanilla extract in a separate bowl until smooth and creamy. Using a wooden spoon, fold the cream into the cream cheese mixture.

5. Add about 20 drops of pink colouring to the cheesecake topping and lightly stir in with a cocktail stick to give a swirly effect. Spoon on top of the biscuit base and carefully smooth into an even layer without losing the pink swirls. Chill for 2 hours to firm up, or overnight if you have time.

6. To serve, remove the outer rim of the cake tin and scatter the chocolate beans over the cheesecake.

Unicorn Sky cake

Reach for the stars with this magical unicorn sky cake. The carrot cake has a creamy, fluffy icing, fondant clouds and white chocolate stars.

Serves: 16
Preparation: 40 minutes, plus chilling
Bake: 1 hour

You will need:

+ 250g self-raising flour
+ Pinch of salt
+ 1 teaspoon cinnamon
+ 1 teaspoon mixed spice
+ 225g light soft brown sugar
+ 250g carrots, peeled and grated
+ 3 large eggs, lightly beaten
+ 200ml sunflower oil

Creamy icing:

+ 100g unsalted butter, softened, plus extra for greasing
+ 175g cream cheese
+ 200g icing sugar, sifted
+ 1 teaspoon vanilla extract

To decorate:

+ 100g white fondant icing
+ Blue, pink and orange gel food colouring
+ Large white chocolate stars
+ Star sprinkles

Special equipment:

+ 20cm square cake tin
+ Cocktail sticks

1. First make the fondant clouds. Split the fondant into three pieces. Add a few drops of blue food colouring to one third of the icing and knead until partly mixed in. Repeat with the orange and pink colouring and the remaining fondant.

2. Sprinkle a little icing sugar over the worktop and roll out the fondant until about 3–4mm thick. Cut out cloud shapes and insert a cocktail stick into the flat base of each one. Let them dry and harden for a few hours, or overnight.

3. Heat the oven to 180C/160C fan/Gas 4 and line the base of the cake tin and grease the sides with butter.

4. Sift the flour, salt, cinnamon and mixed spice into a large mixing bowl. Add the sugar and carrots and mix well.

5. Mix together the eggs and oil in a jug, then pour into the flour mixture and stir with a wooden spoon until combined.

6. Pour the cake mixture into the prepared tin and bake for 55 to 60 minutes until a skewer inserted into the middle comes out clean. Leave to cool in the tin for 10 minutes, then turn out onto a wire rack to cool completely.

7. Meanwhile, make the creamy icing. Beat the butter until really soft, then beat in the cream cheese, sugar and vanilla extract in a bowl until smooth and creamy. Add a few drops of blue food colouring to the frosting and stir in using a cocktail stick to make a swirly pattern. Chill for at least 1 hour to firm up.

8. Spoon the icing over the top of the cake to cover, taking care not to lose the swirly blue pattern. Decorate with the fondant clouds, chocolate stars and sprinkles.

My First Unicorn cake

It takes a little time and effort to make, but your friends and family will be super impressed with this spectacular unicorn cake! The lemon-flavoured pink and vanilla layered sponge is decorated with buttercream icing, marshmallows, rainbow chocolate buttons and an ice cream cone horn coated in colourful sprinkles.

Serves: about 24
Preparation: 3½ hours, plus chilling
Bake: 30 minutes

You will need:

+ 2 unwaxed lemons

+ 400g unsalted butter, softened, cut into pieces, plus extra for greasing

+ 400g caster sugar

+ 6 large eggs

+ 400g self-raising flour, sifted

+ 2 teaspoons baking powder, sifted

+ Large pinch of salt

+ 4 tablespoons whole milk

+ Pink gel food colouring

+ 2 x recipe quantity vanilla buttercream (see page 4)

+ 6 tablespoons blackcurrant jam (or jam of choice)

To decorate:

+ 60g white fondant icing

+ Edible gold powder

+ Black cardboard or fondant

+ Large candy necklace

+ Ice cream cone, base trimmed if needed

+ Coloured sugar strand sprinkles

+ 2 long unicorn-coloured twisted marshmallows

+ Rainbow white chocolate buttons

+ Pink, white, blue and yellow mini marshmallows in various sizes and shapes

Special equipment:

+ 4 x 18cm round cake tins

+ Baking paper

+ 20cm cake board

+ Cake stand (optional)

+ Palette knife or cake scraper

Top Tip!
See page 5 for how to make the unicorn ears and eyes.

1. Make the unicorn ears and eyes following the instructions on page 5, then leave to harden until needed, or overnight.

2. Heat the oven to 200C/180C fan/Gas 6 and line the base of four 18cm cake tins with baking paper and grease the sides.

3. Using the small holes of a grater, finely grate the zest (outer skin) of the two lemons. Squeeze the juice from one lemon, then set aside.

4. To make the cake, beat the butter and caster sugar in a large mixing bowl of a stand mixer, or use an electric hand whisk, for 3 to 5 minutes until pale, creamy and fluffy. You may have to scrape down the sides of the bowl from time to time.

5. Add the eggs, a little at a time, beating well until combined. Don't worry if the mixture curdles a little. Add the flour, baking powder, milk, lemon zest and juice to the mixing bowl and fold in until the cake mixture is smooth and creamy.

6. Divide half the cake mixture between two lined cake tins, about 400g each tin, and level the tops with a palette knife. Add a few drops of the pink colouring to the remaining cake mixture and fold in gently to make a light pink mixture. Spoon the pink cake mixture into the two remaining lined cake tins and level the tops with a palette knife.

7. Bake the cakes for 25 to 30 minutes until risen, golden and a skewer inserted into the middle comes out clean. Leave the cakes in the tins for 5 minutes, then turn out to cool completely on a wire rack.

To make the filling and coating:

8. While the cakes are baking, make the buttercream following the instructions on page 4. (You will need to double the quantity of buttercream for this recipe.)

9. Spoon a quarter of the buttercream into a

bowl, then spoon half of this into a separate bowl. Add about 30 drops of pink food colouring to one of the bowls to make a dark pink and 12 drops to the second bowl to make a pale pink icing, then stir gently to blend in. (Leave the larger quantity of buttercream plain.)

10. If your cakes are domed, use a bread knife to level the top of each cake. Secure one of the plain cakes to the cake board using a little of the plain buttercream.

11. Spoon some of the plain buttercream on top of the cake, around the outer edge, making a 5cm-wide border. Spread two tablespoons of the blackcurrant jam on top of the cake inside the buttercream – the buttercream border will stop the jam running over the edge of the cake.

12. Place a pink sponge on top and repeat with the buttercream and jam. Top with the second plain sponge, then add more

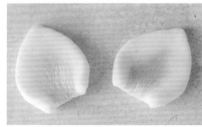

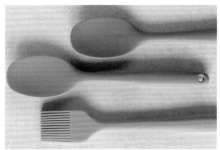

buttercream and jam. Top with the second pink sponge to make a four-tiered cake, alternating plain and pink, then press down lightly.

13. Spread a very thin layer of white buttercream over the top and down the sides of the cake using a palette knife – it doesn't matter if the cake shows through in places – this will give you a good base for a thicker second layer of buttercream. Chill for 1 hour, or overnight if you have time.

14. Now for the final layer of buttercream. First spread the dark pink buttercream around the bottom quarter of the cake using a cake scraper or palette knife to make a smooth, even layer.

15. Next, spread the pale pink buttercream above the dark pink icing, covering a second quarter of the cake. Blend the two shades of pink together with a palette knife or cake scraper.

16. Spread the plain buttercream (saving a little to cover the ice cream cone) over the top and down the sides of the cake until it meets the pale pink buttercream. Using a palette knife or cake scraper, spread the buttercream evenly over the cake. Carefully blend together the three colours of icing to make a smooth coating, then leave for 30 minutes.

To decorate the Unicorn Cake:

17. Time to have fun with the decorations! Place the candy necklace around the bottom of the cake to neaten the edge.

18. To make the unicorn horn, spread the remaining buttercream evenly over the ice cream cone. Put the cone on a plate and

scatter over the coloured sprinkles until coated all over. Carefully press the horn into the centre of the top of the cake – the buttercream should hold it in place. Place the unicorn ears either side of the horn.

19. To make the unicorn mane, cut each long marshmallow into three strips. Place one end of a marshmallow strip near the horn and let it flow over the top and down one side of the cake. Press lightly to stick it to the buttercream. Repeat with the remaining strips of marshmallow, arranging them down the right-hand side and back of the cake.

20. Arrange the rainbow chocolate buttons and the small marshmallows between the long marshmallow strips and on the top and front of the cake to make a unicorn fringe. Press the unicorn eyes below the fringe – they should stick on the buttercream.

Congratulations, you've made your first unicorn cake – now it's time to share it with your friends and family!

★ Index ★